New York.

It's

M000195388

first time driving into Manha... Washington Bridge and slowly approaching the dense skyscrapers rising from the horizon. Welcome to New York City.

Over the years, this place has attracted anyone who's wanted to make it big: from artists and intellectuals, to supermodels and self-proclaimed masters of the universe. The city had it's fair share of ups and downs but it's always managed to get back on its feet.

New York has extended itself to the outer boroughs— it's not just The City anymore. But does Williamsburg as the capital of beards, fixed gears and craft beer really represent the city's identity? And where is Manhattan alive and kicking today?

To answer these questions we spoke with a diverse range of people: parents of eight from Brooklyn, a couple who run a restaurant in SoHo, a Danish artist from Chinatown, a musician from Williamsburg, and a style icon who moved from Belgium 25 years ago.

38HOURS is about the value and worth of the experience. It's about the smell, taste and feel that such experiences conjure up. This guide will hone your sensitivities and improve your level of engagement with the city. In order to do so, we have drawn from our network of locals to guide you through their versions of this effervescent city.

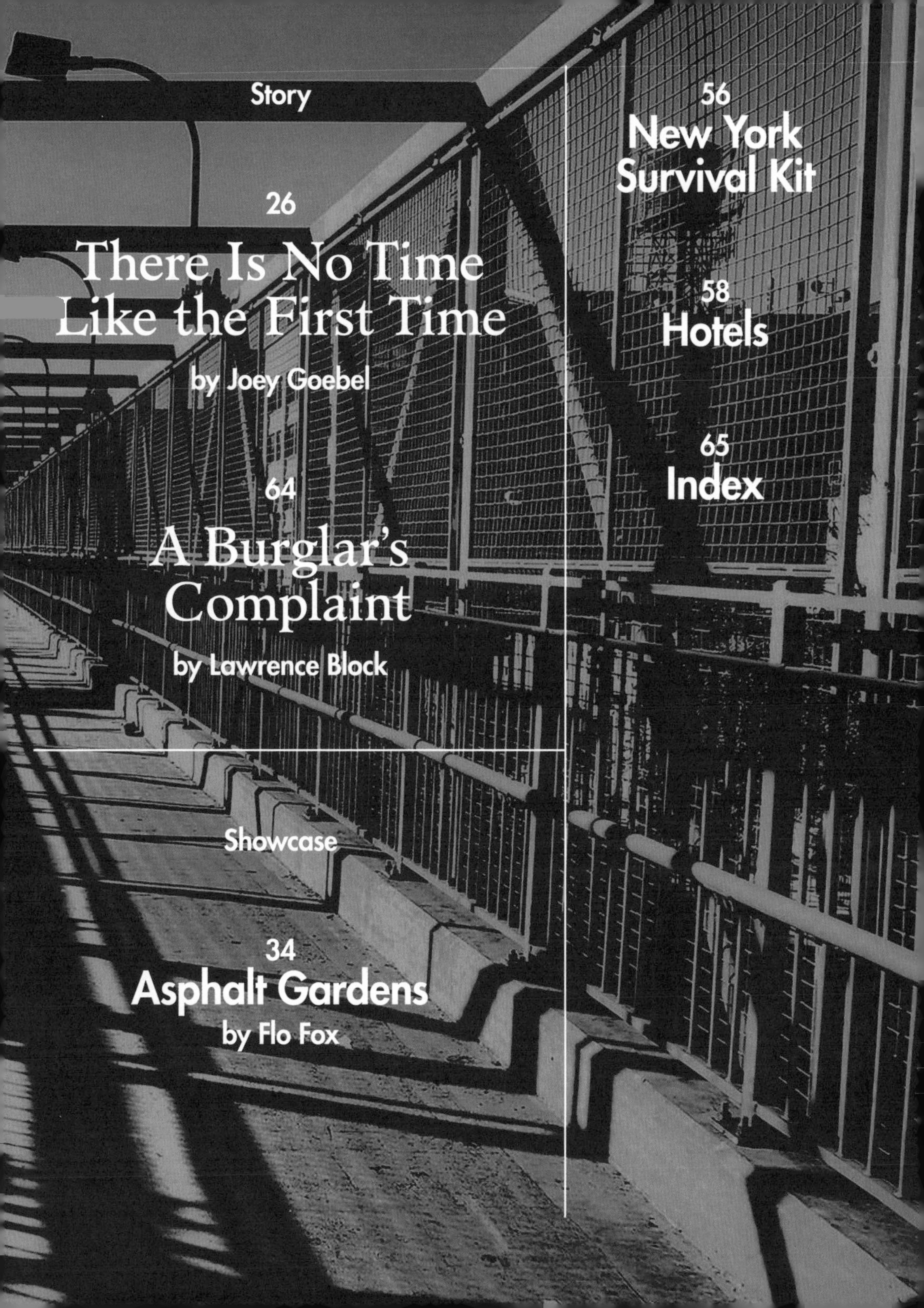

Franklin D. Roosevelt is a giant among American Presidents and ranks among the nation's most beloved. Louis I. Kahn is widely revered as one of the masters of 20th century architecture. The intersection of these two pillars of American society could only result in something spectacular. Four Freedoms Park, the latest addition to NYC green spaces, is a testament to both timeless vision and modernist design. The ideal way to get there is by taking the skytrain, which runs parallel to the

Queensboro bridge. Built in 1976, it initially served as a temporary solution for the absence of a train, but it's since stood the test of time and even been featured in Hollywood blockbusters such as Nighthawk and Léon: The Professional. You can tell the locals apart from the tourists by who is holding to the handrails following the announcement.
• Roosevelt Island Tramway, 59th St. and 2nd Avenue

Surfin' NYC

This may not be the first activity that comes to mind when in New York, but a great way to escape the summer heat is to take the A Train to Rockaway Island. Here you can enjoy the promenade, lounge on the sandy beaches, and yes, spend the afternoon riding some waves. After a full day of splitting peaks, one can stroll down the boulevard to the *Rockaway Beach Inn* for some $2.25 pints and Pogues from the jukebox.
• Rockaway Beach Inn, Queens

From Yachtlike Rooftops to Musical Steakhouses

Bright Lights, Big City

Food · Culture | A Bronx Tale

Italian-Americans are the the largest European ethnic group in the city. A lot of neighbourhoods have their own Little Italy, the one in the Bronx being probably the most well-known. The heart of the community is the *Arthur Avenue Retail Market.* After visiting Café del Mercato or Greco's for a snack, take to the streets and check out shops like *Borgatti's* for homemade pasta or *Calabria* for pancetta and sausages. Or grab lunch at *Tra Di Noi* or *Roberto's.* Then treat yourself to a strong espresso and a long walk in the neighbouring *Botanical Garden* to work off the extra calories.
• Arthur Avenue, Bronx

| Night | On Top of the World

There are over 120 rooftop bars in New York and each has its own character and unique clientele. The in-crowd prefers to enjoy their sundowners with a Manhattan skyline view: on the Brooklyn side *Sheltering Sky* presents a Moroccan ambiance, contemporary DJs and straightforward drinks. In Manhattan's West Village, *Sunsets* in the historical *Jane Hotel* offers a dignified, elegant atmosphere.

Here the star of the show is the bright Hudson River sunset. Complement the view with a smooth "Lavender & White Peach Bellini". For the full flavour of Gotham, head to Midtown: on the 29th floor, atop The Viceroy Hotel, *The Roof* offers a 360-degree view and a yacht-inspired atmosphere. Avoid the weekends when the selfie crowd checks in.
• several locations, see index p. 67

Outdoors | Bushwick's Heart and Soul

New York is widely known as the mecca of street art and it definitely doesn't disappoint. Urban art once was crude, and seen as a form of vandalism, derived from the provocative and relentless gang and anti-establishment culture. Today, with the help of established artists like Banksy, street art has transformed itself from an underground criminal act into a well-respected art form, and a public medium for freedom of speech. A collection of the most impressive and skillful works can be seen in Bushwick, Brooklyn. Get off at Jefferson St. Station and step into the heart of the infamous Bushwick Collective, a conglomerate of artists from the area. Begin your tour on Troutman St. and let the colourful walls lead you through to St Nicholas Ave., Scott Ave. and Jefferson St. You'll be taken aback by the sheer amount of space covered with art. Grab a quick beer at *Heavy Woods* or a coffee in *AP Café* and take a short walk to Meserole through Waterbury and Scholes St., the next street art hub on your tour.
• Bushwick Collective Gallery, Bushwick

Food | Backdoor Dining

Few restaurants have earned a four star rating from The New York Times. *Eleven Madison Park* has managed that feat not once, but twice—which ranks it in the upper echelons of NY's fine dining experiences. It also comes with a price tag and a reservation policy to match. Fortunately the $225 tasting menu and waiting time can be circumvented if you drop in to order à la carte and dine in the restaurant's bar *Nook*. You might not get all the fanfare you'd receive in the main dining room, but the food served will be just as delicious.
• Eleven Madison Park, Midtown, elevenmadisonpark.com

Food | Carnivores United

There are several places in town where you can get a solid piece of meat. But the *Peter Luger Steakhouse* under the Williamsburg Bridge is the only one rated with a Michelin star. The oak furniture gives it a rustic feel and the food speaks for itself. In Manhattan, *Keens Steakhouse* (photo) presents a more distinguished ambiance. Here you can enjoy a perfectly served dry-aged prime Porterhouse steak. And for those who've seen it all: visit *Sammy's* on the Lower East Side to enjoy some whimsical atmosphere and the raucous live gigs of Dani Luv. Soak up the scene while enjoying a tender veal cutlet served by the Jewish-Romanian kitchen.
• several locations, see index p. 67

Outdoors | Garden State

The Big Apple is one of the most densely populated cities in the world—making it near impossible for people to own a garden. New Yorkers have found creative ways around this issue. All over town locals have revamped neglected spaces like unused rooftops, forgotten subway tracks and vacant lots to create new green areas transforming New York into a benchmark for urban farming and gardening. Take a visit to *Eagle Street Rooftop Farm* in Brooklyn which operates its own seasonal farmer's market and even provides supplies to local restaurants. Or go to Alphabet City and get a coffee in the magical and publicly accessible *9th Street Community Garden*. It's the perfect repose from New York's usual hurly-burly.
• several location, see index p. 67

Lena Viddo & Felipe Avalos
Lena is a painter and multimedia
artist of Swedish-Colombian
descent. She represented The
United States at the Florence
Biennale. Felipe was born in New
York City to Cuban and Puerto
Rican parents and has his professional background in gastronomy
and fashion. The couple has
been married since 2007. Together
with their kids they constitute
a family of ten.

Lena Viddo & Felipe Avalos, artist and restaurateur

Full House

Lena and Felipe moved across the bridge to Brooklyn a few years
ago. They're not the biggest fans of local hipsterism there, but they
value the old and classic vibe of the borough. Follow Lena and Felipe
on their path from Uruguayan restaurants to underground parties.

You left SoHo a few years ago—is Manhattan finally over?

Felipe: I felt Manhattan was over 10 years ago, when it stopped being egalitarian—the watermark became not how creative, or cool, or interesting you were, but more what hedge fund or bank you worked for. I tried to get Lena to consider the move but she couldn't come to grips with the fact that Manhattan was dying. I finally got her to agree to move and now she's set up her painting studio in Bushwick and she couldn't be happier.

Lena: Yes, Manhattan is over. It's not totally over yet, but fading fast. It has become a moated kingdom, now only for the uber-wealthy and the occasional straggler. Diversity and art drew me to New York, and sadly the former is almost gone. The island has become a Disney-white, perfectly cleaned-up version of itself. In the 20 years that I lived in SoHo, it went from being a funky, integrated neighbourhood comprised of artists, small business owners, old school Italians, and original oddballs, to a shopping mall of the highest order, encompassed by multi-million dollar lofts sitting empty waiting for their foreign and celebrity owners to come for a visit.

What's still worth crossing the East River for?

Lena: The city still has its magical moments and in terms of culture it continues to deliver.

Felipe: For instance seeing Patti Smith at *Poisson Rouge* or going to see Debbie Harry at *The Carlyle*.

Lena: Those occasions, however, are becoming farther and fewer between, and they seem to be shifting to Brooklyn.

Felipe: It's funny because years ago Manhattanites—I was

one—would get upset about BNT—'Bridge and Tunnel'—people, a term used to describe anyone coming into the city from the outer boroughs. However, now Manhattanites flock to Brooklyn for cool dining, clubbing etc, and are now they're considered the BNT people. Funny how things change.

Lena: The shopping is still better in the city. Although Brooklyn doesn't come close to Manhattan in this regard, it does have what Manhattan lost: the unusual, odd and quirky mom and pop shops that are no longer found in the city.

You live in Williamsburg. This seems to be the global capital of the Hipsters—does it get on your nerves?

Felipe: If I am going to be honest then I must say it does. However, when you live here and you grow up as part of the fabric of what it is to be a real New Yorker, and you see 'carpetbaggers', then its pretty easy to shift through the frauds, fakes and wannabes. A true New York talent is ignoring bullshit and not giving a fuck! Fuck hipsters and their beards. They will move on to some other shit soon enough.

Lena: Yes, it can be annoying in daily life, especially when you roll with a family of eight bickering kids. We are an anomaly in our neighbourhood—and in most for that matter. Our neighbours seem completely perplexed by the unpredictable cast of characters that comprise our family. At this point six of the eight kids are teenagers and older, and none qualify as hipsters. So we get looked at, and the neighbours can't figure out what's going on at our place, where heated verbal sparring in Spanish and a revolving door of kids coming and going are standard daily occurrences. I love all people, however, and hipsters obviously fall into this category.

Momo
Bushwick

Roberta's
Bushwick

The River Café
Dumbo

Di Fara
Outskirts

Nathan's
Outskirts

Bond Street
West Village

Raoul's
Soho

Blue Ribbon Sushi
Soho

Estela
Soho

Minetta Tavern
West Village

Omen
Soho

Fat Radish
West Village

Cook Shop
Chelsea

Jivamukti Café
West Village

One Lucky Duck
Midtown

La Luncheonette
Chelsea

Tabare
Williamsburg

Where in Brooklyn can I still find the old and traditional?

Lena: Although it appears old and traditional, because it's housed in a vintage diner, we love *The Diner*. A pioneer restaurant of Williamsburg, *Marlow and Sons*, has been around since 1998 and also one of our favourites. *Hotel Delmano* is a gorgeous Williamsburg bar for a drink. The area down around the Domino Sugar Factory is coming to life with *Crown Victoria*, which is great on a summer night with outdoor picnic tables for burgers. The roof of the *Whythe Hotel* boasts the best views of the city skyline in Williamsburg. The first neighbourhood I resided in when arriving to NYC for Art School in 1988 was Clinton Hill. My favourite restaurants in Bushwick are *Momo* and *Roberta's*. For a very romantic date *The River Café* is a Brooklyn classic with incredible views of Manhattan.

Felipe: But to really still get the vibe of Old Brooklyn you have to get out to Sheepshead, Benson-hurst, Brighton Beach, Coney Island. To get a slice of heaven you need to go to *Di Fara's* and hope you don't have to wait too long—but you probably will. It may just be a hot hog, but if you haven't tried *Nathan's* on the boardwalk you are definitely missing out!

Felipe, you have a restaurant, and Lena, you're also a connoisseur. What are the most amazing restaurants in NYC from your perspectives?

Felipe: Being in the restaurant business and having had offices in HK and Europe for the better part of 20 years I find it difficult to use the word 'amazing'. I find that amazing is when I dine at a friend's house who cooks with passion and love, pretty much the way I do. There are several places Lena and I have been going religiously for

almost 20 years though, which means they must be pretty good, having stood the test of time. Places like *Bond Street*, *Raoul's*, *Blue Ribbon Sushi*. New ones have come onto the scene that deserve much attention also, such as my friend and very talented chef Ignacio Matto's relatively new spot *Estela* in Nolita, where President Obama and the First Lady dined not too long ago. *Minetta Tavern* also should be mentioned as a place that will still deserve to be amongst the best 10 years down the road.

Lena: I still have some old school favourites in Soho, like *Omen* for soba noodles and sashimi and *Blue Ribbon* for sushi. Serge and Karim Raoul's classic French brasserie *Raoul's* still maintains a strong foothold in Soho. Its been a regular haunt of ours for over 25 years. My favourite neighbourhood in Manhattan is the Lower East Side below Delancey Street, and there we love *Fat Radish* for market-to-table. When we're in Chelsea for an opening *Cook Shop* offers fresh farm-to-table fare. *Jivamukti Café* and *One Lucky Duck* are my favourites for a fast lunch after yoga, and *Jivamukti* is my favourite drop-in yoga studio in Manhattan. *La Luncheonette* is a secret little classic spot in West Chelsea that has been around for at least 25 years as well.

You both have Latin backgrounds—where could one find "Sabor Latino" in New York?

Lena: For Sabor Latino, we always have something going on, as the majority of our friends are Latino and Brazilian. At *Tabare* in Williamsburg we can always find a handful of our sophisto-funky urban Uruguayan, Argentinian and Colombian friends who regularly hang there, so we love it and the community created by Diego and

Bruno, the owners who've been together for over 20 years. These boys know how to have a good time and serve delicious organic Uruguayan treats. In the city, the best place for an intimate latin music venue remains *SOB's*. It's tricky though—you really have to know who's performing because otherwise the crowd can get rough. We recently went with our Cuban and Colombian friends to a weekly Cuban Santeria jam in the West Village at *Zinc Bar*, a dive bar on 3rd st. It was super alternative and of course it's why we live in New York. Food wise we can also recommend *Papatzul* for Mexican and *Casa* on Bedford for Brazilian food.

Felipe: For an old-school Puertorican—no-frills yet deliciously authentic and unimaginably inexpensive—meal go to *La Taza de Oro* in West Village. If you're feeling adventurous go to *Cositas Ricas* in Queens where you will swear you landed in Medellín for a fabulous Bandeja Paisa served.

Lena, you are a painter... is the NYC art scene still loud? Which galleries and events would you recommend to get an insight?
Lena: The art scene is tricky. For me, the cool things are always the outliers, alternative and non-commercial events that friends and artists are holding. *Pioneer Works* art centre in Red Hook is amazing and worth the trip. It's a gorgeous space inside of an old factory with artist residencies, classes and interesting shows. I also like Manish Vora's events and non-commercial shows in and around town.

You are such a big family. You have eight children and some still live with you. Where do you go to entertain the little ones?
Lena: There are so many places for families to take kids, including all of the museums and parks in Brooklyn. We go to the movies at the *Bushwick Inlet Park* in Williamsburg, or just walk the streets of Brooklyn. A day at the *Brooklyn Museum* and *Botanical Gardens* is highly recommended and Park Slope or Crown Heights afterwards for lunch. *Brooklyn Flea* and *Smorgasbord* in combination with Bushwick Inlet Park is a regular outing for our posse. The *Children's Museum* in Soho is great on a rainy day.

Lena, if your friends from Sweden are visiting and they want to go shopping, where do you take them?
Lena: When my Swedish friends and family come to visit I recommend for my young, artsy nieces and nephews *Mary Meyer Vintage* for eclectic and inexpensive accessories and random vintage. *Bond 07* by Selima is the best in town for very rare, upscale vintage and quirky independent designers, not to mention original fashion-forward eyewear. *The Hat Shop* on Thompson is a gem for eccentric and classic hats by independent milliners. *BLK DNM* on Lafayette in Soho has something cool and edgy for all ages. *IF* boutique on Grand offers edgy, modern and forward accessories by independent jewelry designers and some super cool handbags, key chains and wallets. *Oak* on Bond Street is great for shoes.

If you had 24 hours without kids and wanted to spend a romantic day and evening, where would you go, what would you do?
Lena: Once upon a time, long ago we enjoyed checking into *The Pierre*. We loved to order room service, eat in, have some fun, spend time in Central Park and get a massage in the morning. Lately, we have opted for wilder and less sophis-

Authentic Uruguayan cuisine in Williamsburg: Tabare

ticated outings, which include dancing until dawn. For real romance we leave town without the children.

Felipe: When we can, our idea of a 24-hour romantic getaway is being able to dance all night at a *Robot Heart* party at an undisclosed underground warehouse somewhere in Brooklyn, enjoying the sounds of an internationally acclaimed DJ who flew in from Ibiza to spin. We leave when the sun is up and grab a bite and a beer before comfortably settling back into our role as parents of eight.

On really hot summer days, what's the best beach that's reachable within an hour from here?

Lena: I personally love *Asbury Park*, which is a little bit over an hour away from the city. It's run down and eclectic, but like everything else getting gentrified by the minute. The crowd can be sketchy, but the abandoned buildings along the beach are worth the trip.

Felipe: Yes, Asbury Park, it is also hometown of the legendary Bruce Springsteen and his E Street Band. Just cruise the boardwalk and grab a bite at *Porta*.

Greenpoint & Long Island City
A Point of View

The whole world seems to be talking about Brooklyn. Williamsburg has been written about ad infinitum, but it's grittier neighbours to the north, Greenpoint and Long Island City, are also worthy of discovery.

Outdoors | **Almost Yachtrock**

By far, the most convenient and exciting way to arrive in the outer boroughs is by the East River Ferry. The ferry, as its name suggests, travels the East River, providing a connecting service between Midtown Manhattan and Wall Street, via stops in Brooklyn and Queens. In Brooklyn's earliest days, Greenpoint was mainly farmland, before it became industrialised. These days when arriving at the India Street/Greenpoint ferry landing, one doesn't only find a vibrant residential neighbourhood, but also a popular community which is home to a mix of artists and musicians, blue-collar workers, and creative retailers. With a day-pass one could continue the ride, which provides gorgeous views of the legendary Manhattan skyline, NY Harbor, Lady Liberty, and the quartet of lower East River bridges. In Dumbo one should visit the Jean Nouvel-designed glass enclosure that houses *Jane's Carousel* in Brooklyn Bridge Park. In short, the ferry provides an angle of New York City that you won't get standing atop a skyscraper, riding the subway, or walking its bustling streets.

• East River Ferry, eastriverferry.com

Shop | Made in Brooklyn

There's more than a handful of people crazy about denim and fanatic for selvedge fabrics. Words and phrases like artisanal, heritage, craftsmanship and attention to detail roll trippingly from their tongues. If these words speak to you, then *Loren* is the place you need to see. From fabric to finish Loren specializes in hand-crafted premium denim. This Brooklyn-based boutique-cum-workshop offers a rare look into the craftsmanship behind small-batch, handmade jeans. Choose from any of a number of finely selected brands or splurge and get measured for a custom pair of your own.
• Loren, 80 Nassau Ave., Greenpoint, lorencronk.com

Food | Sustainable Seafood

For a clump of islands located on the shore of the Atlantic, NYC rarely feels like a harbour town. That makes finding a great seafood restaurant where you feel transported to Maine all the more special. Greenpoint may be located at water's edge, but it's certainly more known for pierogies and kielbasa than fried oysters and sea urchin. Proprietors Adam Geringer-Dunn and Vinny Milburn have made it their mission to introduce high-quality, sustainable, local seafood to the neighbourhood. Beyond the restaurant, there's a retail fish market, spices, cookbooks, and salt water taffies.
• Greenpoint Fish & Lobster Co., 114 Nassau Ave., Greenpoint, greenpointfish.com

Night | Rescued and Restored

With Brooklyn's rapid development, it's easy to forget its gritty nautical past. At *Achilles Heel*, the latest venture from Brooklyn maestro restaurateur Andrew Tarlow, the waterfront once again plays centre stage. This corner space existed as a neighbourhood tavern for 60 years, but sat vacant for over forty. Original mirrors and a well-worn hardwood bar evoke the past that once catered to needy dockworkers. Enjoy a natural wine or find salvation in a perfectly pulled espresso. The bar may have been refurbished and restored, but it still has that old-world, worn-in feel.
• Achilles Heel, 180 West Street, Greenpoint, achillesheelnyc.com

A Point of View

Food Old Fashioned

Greenpoint has been categorised as a Polish neighbourhood, rich in culture and neighbourhood pride, with a desire to maintain its identity; no matter how popular it gets. Named for the borough across the river, Manhattan Avenue, Greenpoint's main thoroughfare, is characteristically Brooklyn through and through, lined with butchers and businesses many of which have been there since the 1950s. One such business, *Peter Pan*, serves classic donuts that are consistently ranked among the city's best. The countertop seating, uniforms and signs have not changed, and the same could be said for some of its longstanding clientele.

• Peter Pan, 727 Manhattan Ave., Greenpoint

Night Music and Lights

As Williamsburg goes the way of the Meatpacking district, it's inevitable that the cutting edge party would also move on. Enter *Good Room*, a dance club operated by stalwart nightlife veterans. The 5,000 square foot space has a dedicated vinyl room—decorated in an industrial library style setting with exposed brick, glass cabinets, and vinyl discs lining the shelves. An adjacent lounge is dedicated to softer tunes. The club is raw but sophisticated, replete with the requisite bombastic sound system and the obligatory state-of-the-art lighting, smoke machines and disco ball.

• The Good Room, 98 Meserole Ave., Greenpoint, goodroombk.com

Food Gourmet Vikings

Brooklyn's newest Michelin star restaurant is served with a decidedly Danish twist. The restaurant serves fare courtesy of Chef Daniel Burns, formerly of Copenhagen's renowned Noma. Luksus is located in the back of Tørst, possibly the most imaginative beer bar in Brooklyn. Behind a sliding door at the rear of the bar, sits a 26-seat tasting-menu-only restaurant. Like the room of all blond Scandinavian timber, the courses served are nothing short of elegant and refined. Request a seat at the kitchenside counter, where Burns performs as your de facto dinner companion.

• Luksus at Tørst, 615 Manhattan Ave., Greenpoint, luksusnyc.com

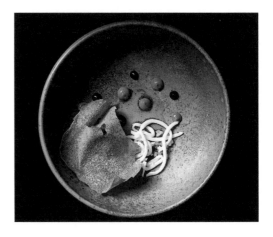

| Culture | **Creative Hub** |

Manhattan isn't the only cluster of high culture to be found in NYC. On the other side of Newton Creek, the waterway which divides Brooklyn from Queens, is Long Island City. LIC, as it's abbreviated, is home to many world-class institutions, chief among them, The Noguchi Museum. It was founded and designed by Isamu Noguchi, for the display of what he considered to be representative examples (photo) of his oeuvre. Housed in a converted industrial building, containing an interior garden of Noguchi's own design, the museum itself is considered to be one of the artist's finest works. Noguchi, an early pioneer, led the metamorphosis of LIC into the arts district it is today, which includes MoMA PS1. PS1 is one of the oldest and largest nonprofit contemporary art institutions in the United States. An exhibition space rather than a collecting institution, PS1's mission is to display the most experimental art in the world. A former public elementary school, PS1 presents its diverse program in an environment that is both unique and welcoming. Additionally, Museum of the Moving Image is America's only museum dedicated to the art, history, technique, and technology of the moving image in all its forms. For connoisseurs of classic cinema to generations of avid gamers, the Museum of the Moving Image is a one-of-a-kind destination for audiences of all ages and interests.

• Long Island City, serveral locations, see Index p. 67

Endless Inspiration

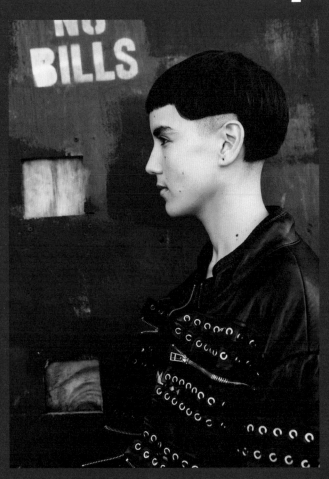

Kim Ann Foxman
firstly came into global recognition as a singing member of the famed house and neo-disco band Hercules And Love Affair. After she stepped away from singing with the New York-based collective she ennobled tracks by prominent dance music producers Kink and Maya Jane Coles with her deeply touching voice. She also travels the world as the sought-after DJane and plays regularly in major-league clubs like Berghain, in Berlin and Fabric, in London. In 2014 she launched her very own record label, Firehouse, under which she debuted her record It's All About You.

What does the heartbeat of New York City look like, taste like and sound? What should someone wear, eat, or listen to in order to feel at home there? New York-based DJ, singer and producer Kim Ann Foxman blows the whistle on some secret shopping spots, tells us the best places to go for tasty New York eats, and tunes us in to the

You originally lived in San Francisco. What made you come to New York, and how did the city welcome you?

I'm actually from Hawaii. I was born and raised in Hawaii, then I moved to San Francisco where I went to college. I lived there for seven amazing years before I made the move to New York City in 2002. I was in a relationship at the time, which was what led me to NYC. I was ready for a change and it was all so exciting for me.

What was your musical taste like when you were younger?

I grew up loving R'n'B and radio hip hop. Also a lot of Latin freestyle, reggae and early Jamaican dancehall, which was really popular growing up on an island like Hawaii.

Can you describe to us the inspiration behind your label Firehouse?

I chose the name because I actually live in an old firehouse in the Brooklyn neighborhood. I also have my studio there, which is where I produce my music, so the name fits perfectly.

How does living in NYC shape your work as a DJ and producer?

It shapes me because it inspires me constantly. I love the city and its energy. It's filled with so many talented people who are constantly giving me new ideas. I find it really motivating.

What are three albums that you'd recommend to someone who wants to really connect with NYC through music?

There are way too many to cut it down to only three, but here are some that come to mind straight away: ESG, "ESG"—released by the legendary post-punk and avant-garde label 99 Records in 1981. Pure dance-punk, funk and no wave energy, tuned by an all-female quintet. They were one of the most dynamic bands that New York had to offer at the height of the 1980s.

Eric B and Rakim, "Paid In Full"—this is the debut album of the NYC hip hop duo from Long Island. Some say they've been one of the most influential DJ/MC combos of all time. Rakim's stoic, free-rhythm rapping style and the gritty, heavy beats are representative of the heartbeat of NYC until today.

Arthur Russell, "The World of Arthur Russell"—a compilation released by the London-based label Soul Jazz Records. A great summary of Arthur Russell's danceable work that was highly influential on New York's underground dance and disco scene throughout the late 1970s and early 1980s. On this compilation you find tracks like Go Bang, In The Cornbelt, or It Is All Over My Face, which were big hits in legendary clubs like Paradise Garage or The Loft. They had a big influence on the genesis of house music. Essential emotional New York City music that moves your soul deeply.

If you would travel in time: in which period would you like to live in NYC and why?

Of course I would wish to be in the 1980s in New York. It's the New York that everyone romanticises, as it was the heyday for so many genres of music... and wild and carefree nightlife. There were legendary clubs like The Loft or Paradise Garage that you can't find in contemporary New York anymore. Also legendary DJs like Larry Levan, Nicky Siano and Frankie Knuckles, who were essential to the origin of house music, were active in that time and played at those clubs.

Is NYC still the city that never sleeps?

I think so. I can really feel it when I visit other places and want to eat something, but it's too late—everything is closed! In New York City we're spoiled for choice, especially for late night good food options, and there are so many 24-hour delis in each borough. You can also get the train around the whole city 24 hours a day, which is very cool. Cities like London do not have such a service. The clubs may not stay open as late as in other cities, but there's still always some action happening. I think it's great to have options all the time!

And is high-priced NYC still good for subcultural movements? If so, where do they happen currently?

Sure. There are a lot of underground parties happening in Brooklyn. There is the *Output Club*, which has a really great programme with an international DJ roster. Another venue is *Verboten* which also offers house and techno from around the world and has a restaurant too. But these are the established names. There are also lots of little spaces and parties in secret locations happening in Brooklyn.

What's your favourite place to watch over the city?

I love the *High Line*. It's a 1.45-mile-long linear aerial greenway and rails-to-trails park on an elevated section of a disused New York central railroad spur that was once called The West Side Line. It extends from Gansevoort Street to 34th Street and even though it doesn't tower above everything per se, the view is awesome and it's really pretty.

What are your top five stores in NYC and where can we find them?

Opening Ceremony in Chinatown has a multinational approach to retail and it also features many homegrown designers. As well as selling clothes, they also offer a great range of accessories. I also like to stroll around *The Strand Bookstore*. It's a classic for New York. The original store opened in 1927. It's an independent bookstore that's located in the East Village. The family business' slogan is "18 Miles Of Books"—which is literally true, as you can find all sorts of books any subject you can imagine. Also *Printed Matter* in Chelsea is great. It is a non-profit organization which is focusing on artist publications. Also art exhibitions and art events are held here. For music, I have to recommend *A1 Records* in the East Village—probably one of the best secondhand vinyl stores around the globe. You can find treasures of all genres, from jazz, funk and soul, to early house and hip hop. Fresh vintage records arrive every day and the prices are very fair. I also like *10 Ft. Single* by Stella Dallas in Williamsburg. It's a carefully curated thrift store that offers very special vintage clothes and accessories from all decades.

Can you name us your favourite restaurants too and tell us what makes them unique?

Allswell in Williamsburg. It's a cozy restaurant with a relaxed feel. The menu changes daily depending on what is available at the farmer's market. That's why they always serve nice, fresh food! It's great for breakfast. *Roberta's Pizza* in Bushwick is my favourite pizza place. I love the Bee Sting pizza, which is spicy and also has honey in it! For amazing noodles I like *Momofuku*. There are three more Momofuku restaurants in Manhattan—it's been named as one of

The original entrance for this Bushwick institution: Roberta's. It's what's inside that counts.

Dimes
Chinatown

The World's 50 Best Restaurants. And for really tasty, healthy vegetarian food, I like *Dimes* in Chinatown. They serve delicious fresh juice and açaí from Brazil. As they open at 8 a.m., it's also great for breakfast.

Biking has become hip in NYC, too. Would you recommend that someone rent one and ride around the town? If so, what's the best route?

Yeah, it's more and more popular over here. I have had a lot of fun biking over the Williamsburg Bridge from Brooklyn to Manhattan and going all the over the town to the water on the West Side. Here you also have the Hudson River Greenway, which is the longest biking route in NY. I hear it runs from the West Side up to West Harlem.

And if someone wants to explore NYC walking, what parts would you recommend?

I like to walk from the East Village down to the Lower East Side, right into Soho and down to Chinatown. This could make for a very nice walking day, giving an excellent impression of what New York City is all about. If that isn't enough, I would suggest walking through parts of the West Side too. For a real long excursion I sometimes like to walk from the East Village all the way up to Central Park. It's nice to see the changes between the areas. It's a long walk but when you do it you experience New York fully.

Finally—is it also true that in NYC the whole world comes to you?

In terms of multiculturalism, yes. But you have to work your ass off here. This city and all it has to offer doesn't come for free! Having said that though, there are loads of opportunities to make it in New York, and it's a blessing to live in such a multicultural place.

There Is No Time Like the First Time

Joey Goebel

The feeling I got the first time I went to New York City is a feeling I doubt I will ever be able to replicate. It was a feeling of wonder that had been out of reach for me since childhood, when Santa and summer vacations were capable of giving me a natural buzz that I had assumed adults are incapable of knowing. It turns out they can know it, if only they go to the great big playground for adults that is New York City.

I come from a town you've never heard of in a state that you make fun of. Henderson, Kentucky might just be the exact opposite of New York City, and this contrast contributed to the sense of wonder the city gave me the first time I went. The occasion was for my honeymoon—the first ten days of a marriage that would ultimately fail (Great Recession, mental illness, etc).

My bride and I had a thing for hotels—something about walking down those long hallways gave us the feeling that life could still hold good things—and the honeymoon was an excuse to stay at not one but two famous ones: The Algonquin and The Hotel Chelsea.

As our taxi left the airport, I'll never forget the first image New York offered us: giant graffiti on the side of a building told us to "QUIT SCHOOL. HAVE SEX." At the time I found this tacky, but now that I've seen what a master's degree can do for one's career (nothing), I see the wisdom in the author's words.

Our cabbie drove as though the lines dividing the lanes were only suggestions, and in half an hour we were in the darkened lobby of The Algonquin. The Algonquin appears to be a quint-essential Midtown Manhattan affair with its green awnings outside and quirks within (New Yorker cartoon wallpaper and a resident cat lounging around wherever she pleases). It is known for its Algonquin Round Table, a group of elitist 1920s writers, including Dorothy Parker, who regularly met there to dine and make fun of people. I couldn't help but feel intelligent in the dim, dignified lobby.

My favourite moment at the Algonquin was when, after getting settled into our nice but nondescript room, I opened the window, and though the only things I could see were the bricks of the next building, I could hear the city. Nothing too special, just sirens and cars passing by—but that's when it sank in: I was here, finally, in this place where everything on Earth that's worth anything seems to happen.

New York City was right outside that window.

The next morning I awakened with a ghastly head cold that I likely acquired on the airplane. The worst cold of my life, in obscenely hot weather, in one of the most crowded cities in the country. And yet, with my first-time-in-New York giddiness, I remember it now as one of my all-time greatest illnesses. This cold could not keep me down, and every time my wife and I stepped out of our hotel and onto the sidewalk, it felt like stepping into pure possibility.

As you might expect, it was not the touristy destinations that made for the best memories on our excursions. New York City's best gifts on that trip came in the form of surprises. For instance, I encountered:

A New York City cop noticing and complimenting my Dead Milkmen T-shirt.

Sailors standing outside of a bar, unabashedly enjoying the sight of female passersby. (It was Fleet Week.)

The smell of barbecue. It led us into a restaurant serving ribs that rivaled Kentucky's, which saddened me a bit.

The man with a horse-pulled carriage shouting, "Hey! You guys wanna have a borderline romantic experience?"

Blisters on my feet. I learned the hard way that Chuck Taylors are not ideal for the NYC pavement and had to buy tennis shoes at a shoe store in Times Square.

Seeing that there really were ducks in the pond at Central Park, just like in The Catcher in the Rye.

The quote of the trip: "You guys wanna walk to Mars or fly to Mars?" The question came from a Puerto Rican cashier clearly sick of her job at Mars 2112, an outer-space themed restaurant where you could simply walk into the dining room or be "flown" there in a minivan-like simulator. (We flew.)

And my favourite moment: we went walking without any destination in mind, holding hands. We lazily turned a corner, and—holy shit!—I saw a sight that had been on my TV a thousand times before: a marquee saying "Late Show with David Letterman." Dave was my comedic hero, and this surprise encounter with the fabled Ed Sullivan Theatre taught me that obsessively planning out our days in order to appease a self-imposed pressure to enjoy, enjoy, enjoy, was the incorrect way to visit New York City.

During our last night at the Algonquin, in hopes of wiping out my cold, I ordered a hot toddy at the hotel bar, the chic but not-stuffy Blue Bar. Miraculously, it worked. I felt fine the next day as we checked into the Hotel Chelsea, entirely different in its vibe to the Algonquin, forgoing classiness in favour of eccentricity. Being a writer and former punk singer, I couldn't resist booking a room at a place where so many artists, writers, and musicians have either stayed or lived, and, yes, where Sid and Nancy's relationship came to its conclusion.

The Hotel Chelsea is almost too cool, but not to the point of being intimidating. Its lobby is what you would expect: mismatched art on the walls, mismatched hipsters in the sitting area. After being checked in by the friendly manager (at that time it was Stanley Bard), we passed a large portrait of Marlon Brando as the Godfather on the floor our room was on.

I thought the room was fine. My wife did not. Admittedly, it did not have the sterile cleanliness that you might find at a Hilton.

She considered it too outdated, leading to the first fight of our marriage.

"This hotel was good enough for Bob Dylan," I said. "It was good enough for Mark Twain. But it's not good enough for you?"

"Well, it probably was good enough for Mark Twain... in 1900."

We ended up going to that omnipresent Manhattan drugstore, Duane Reade, where my wife got flip-flops to wear in the bathroom and various disinfectants. These precautions were not necessary, though, and as we settled in that night and watched TV (the local station played reruns of The Wonder Years all evening long), we were able to laugh at the whole situation. We were also able to laugh at the fact that Mr. Bard was only able to give the honey-mooners a room with two small beds—not that it mattered.

By this point, my wife was wretchedly sick with a head cold of her own, but we still managed to venture out. Now that we felt it was better to happen upon places rather than seek them out, we discovered a new favourite restaurant while staying at the Hotel Chelsea in just the same way. Right across the street was a trailer-park themed restaurant called Trailer Park Lounge & Grill that served sloppy joes, tater tots, and Pabst Blue Ribbon beer. We relished the idea of commoditising white trash culture; I myself had sung for a punk band named the Mullets. We had to ask the waitress, "Are there even any actual trailer parks anywhere near New York City?" (There weren't.) We invited her to come to Kentucky if she ever wanted to experience the real thing. (She didn't.)

Before we knew it, we were back amidst the authentic trailer parks of Kentucky, both of us perfectly healthy once the honey-moon was over. Despite our setbacks, I remember that first trip to New York City as one of my few experiences as an adult in which reality was able to contend with expectations. All my life I had been continually told how this was the greatest place on Earth—and the city actually delivered, despite such a colossal promise.

I once asked myself, "The magic of our childhood—where does it go to when we start to grow up? Does it transfer over to the next generation of children? Or does it just disappear?"

Neither. I witnessed the answer on that first trip. It all ends up in the atmosphere of New York City.

Joey Goebel is an American author from Kentucky. He gained international reputation—especially in Europe—with his novels The Anomalies, Torture the Artist and Commonwealth. The German newspaper Die Welt says about Goebel: "There is hope as long as we have young writers like Joey Goebel."

Natalie Joos, fashion consultant and style icon

Rare Vintage

Natalie Joos
The competitive nature of NYC
requires an individual to
possess more than a single
skill. On Broadway, if you are
a talented actor, singer, and
dancer, you're known as the
triple threat. At the intersection
of social media and fashion,
you'll find Natalie Joos: writer,
stylist, and photographer. A
former casting director for the
likes of Philip Lim and Hugo
Boss, Natalie has gone on to
become a street style darling
and a social media star.

There probably isn't a city in the world with more famous streets than New York. Those streets hold within them a sense of surprise and wonder for those daring enough to take them on. Luckily they've always been open to imports. Natalie Joos has not only conquered the city's mean streets, but she's managed to do it with impeccable style.

The rare bird is the native New Yorker? Are you the rarest of those birds?

I am originally from Belgium, but I've been here so long that I can call myself a New Yorker. I arrived in September of 1997 with two suitcases. I got off the bus in Chinatown and never went back.

What brought you to NYC?

I met a girl in London, where I was studying at the time, who asked me to do her PR in New York. She was an American girl who studied at Central Saint Martin's, who already had a store in Little Italy—so I went.

What changes have you seen since arriving?

Well, all the drug dealers are gone on my block. I mean, New York changes every single day. When I'm gone for more than two weeks, I will walk down the street to get my coffee, and all of a sudden see a whole new building, or a restaurant I've never been to, or an entire flagship store that has moved a block. It's always moving and shaking here.

You settled in Williamsburg before the big rush of gentrification? Can you tell me why there? Why then?

I was living in an apartment in Nolita when I met my now ex-husband. We had two roommates and we thought it was time to settle somewhere together. Brooklyn was kind of up and coming and we heard there was much more space and that rent was much cheaper so we looked all over—Fort Greene, Cobble Hill—and eventually found the perfect two-bedroom in Williamsburg. It was the first new building in the area because as soon as I mentioned the location, people knew what building I meant: "Oh that new building!"

I love my place; I haven't moved since.

Above and beyond the obvious, what do you love about the new times and what do you miss from the old times?

I actually loved the old times much better, when it was still gritty and interesting. There were some crazy bars and the delis were locked up at night. You had to wait behind bulletproof glass. Dealers were 'posted up' in the vestibules of every apartment building—but they were nice. It was lively. I didn't like the hipster movement as much. When everything started changing. But that's the great thing about New York; it's in constant movement, never the same. So when you think something's not right, the next day might be completely different. You have to keep an open mind and adapt. Because in the end it's about how you integrate and create your own little world inside of that big Big Apple.

I gather that you're also a bit of a risk taker and don't mind being out in front of a trend. Could you tell us what you do and how that spirit informs your work?

What I do? So many things. Maybe too many. But I would say styling and writing are my main gigs right now, with photography a close second, or third, to be correct. Im not really that big of a risk taker. I think I just don't want to be like other people. I am curious and am always looking for the next big thing, the thing that will set me apart from the rest and surprise people. My curiosity and urge to be different sometimes puts me ahead of the curve. Especially in fashion. I've launched a few trends. I was also at Coachella for example in 2003, the second festival they ever did. I like discovering new designers, etc.

Who are the NYC designers that the world needs to discover?

Tanya Taylor, Rosie Assoulin and Tim Coppens should be at the top of everyone's list.

How would you define your personal style?

I dress in characters. I can go from 50s housewife to English tomboy with the drop of a hat, literally. But there are a few adjectives that always fit the bill: positive, colourful, sexy, effortless, feminine. I usually dress for the boys.

Where do you go shopping in NYC?

Barneys and *Bergdorf's* shoe floor!

What's the NYC fashion scene like now?

Same as ever, I would say. Loads of shows and designers packed on top each other. Lots of creativity, harnessed by commerce and social media. All in all, New York is still the place where young designers can try to make it. New York is the type of place where everyone puts their best foot forward. Everyone tries to look good and make a mark. You can get inspired just by standing on the corner of North 7th and Bedford, or by the Mercer Hotel in SoHo. I was talking to a girl from LA the other day who wants to make a move to New York. I asked her if she has an agent and she said she would be looking. I told her that she would get noticed just by walking around and within minutes someone would approach her to 'do something'. She'd be connected in no time, I told her. It's so easy in New York. I wouldn't say the fashion scene is as experimental as London, but really, nothing is too crazy for New York. In terms of young talent I think New York is the number one city, but it's not the most prestigious or

exciting in terms of glamour. You have to cross the pond to Europe for that.

Where do all the cool fashion kids hang out?

If I had to venture a guess I would say maybe *Saturdays*, the surf shop, or at *Output* in Williamsburg, *Jack's Wife Freda*... There are many cliques in New York and unfortunately I am not part of any of them anymore since I am way too old (laughs).

When you're not playing 'fashion dress-up' what's your downtime like? How do you spend your days off and where do you go? Does such a thing exist for you?

I love TV and Netflix. I actually still go to the video store! There's a great independant one on Berry Street in Williamsburg called *Videology*. They also have a functioning bar in front which I find quite amusing. I love going to the movies. Walking around with my sister, ironing my laundry while listening to the old school hip-hop station. Running! I love running and pilates. I travel like a maniac, so the times I am not working, I'm usually on a plane or touring a city. I also go on dates as often as I can. I signed up for a few of those online apps and have been meeting guys. It's a lot of fun and it's also interesting. These days it beats going to fashion events!

Can you suggest a nice spot for a date?

I take my dates to *SoHo House* often. Or *Rye* (downstairs). Or *Woodhull*. The last one I took to *Achilles Heel* in Greenpoint. That was nice!

Favourite movie theatre?

In the East Village, *City Cinemas Village East* looks like an old

On Natalia's list when friends from Europe are visiting: The beach in Coney Island.

theatre. It's crumbling and sometimes the movies won't play or the electricity won't work, but it's old school and you know how I love retro...

I know you love retro and vintage. Can you give me the name of a few great vintage stores?

In Williamsburg there's *Amarcord, Stella Dallas* and *Artists & Fleas*. These are all within walking distance from one another. There's also *Pink Clouds* in Little Italy, *Allan & Suzi, Marlene Wetherell, Ritual*, and another branch of *Amarcord* in SoHo.

A great place to buy magazines?

There's a great place on Hudson Street in Greenwich Village called *Casa Magazine* that has every magazine imaginable.

Final question: If you had someone visiting NYC for just 38 hours, what are the things that you would insist that they see or do?

I would have them eat at *Red Rooster* in Harlem and make sure they take some time to visit the *Malcolm Shabazz Market* beforehand. Ride citibikes from Battery Park all the way up the West Side Highway. Have breakfast at *Balthazar*. Visit Coney Island. Definitely see the *Guggenheim*. Get manis and pedis somewhere, especially the Europeans. Go to the food market in Dumbo on the weekend in the summer.

Asphalt Gardens

A showcase by Flo Fox

With her camera she is a witness of the ever changing New York City. Since 1972 Flo shot over 120,000 images and her work is part of the permanent collection of the Smithsonian. Flo is also an advocate for the disabled and taught the first photography class for blind and visually impaired students in 1979.

Asger Carlsen, artist

Inside Out

Asger Carlsen
Started out as a photographer specialising in raw depictions of crime scenes. His aim was to stay as true to reality as possible while exploring photography in an unexpected and unconventional way. In 2006, Carlsen began layering images on top of one another. He was initially shocked by the results—odd-looking faces with many eyes—but he soon came to terms with the unusual technique. Today, Carlsen is known for deconstructions that question both the meaning of photography as well as the prevailing notions of normality and beauty. His sources of inspiration are varied, from surrealist artists like Francis Bacon, to everyday New York, to his bathroom floor.

New York City evokes many connotations. References to the metropolis are ubiquitous—it's featured in songs, movies, books and myths the world over. Yet the city provides a different experience for each individual: a collection of unique expectations, aspirations, disappointments and discoveries. We sat down with Danish artist Asger Carlsen, who has lived in New York for eight years, to discuss his early days in the city, his attachment to Chinatown, and his favourite sanctuary in a Russian spa.

What made you move to New York City?

It was a random decision that came about in 2006. I was working more commercially back then and my New York-based agency gave me a work permit, so I gave it a try.

And you've been here for eight years now. Was it your initial plan to stay for so long?

I didn't really have a schedule. But it quickly became clear to me that it was hard to say whether I would stay for one year, three years or more. It's not easy to survive in New York City. Most people come here and try to make it in the field they want to work in. Maybe they succeed. But if not, there really is not much purpose to being here. You don't just move to New York to enjoy life in a nice apartment with a view of a great park.

You have obviously found your purpose. What do you find so special about New York City?

New York City is an interesting and tough place to live. You can't really afford to be lazy. I hear assumptions about the mentality of people in Berlin—that they have so much time, don't get out before noon and don't actually work. I don't know if this description really reflects the Berlin mentality—it's what I hear—but that is impossible in New York. People really have to do work. They say there's a New York energy. I feel it.

Is it the energy of mega-cities? Do you feel this energy in other big cities?

New York only. The city is unique; especially for its population. There are so many nationalities in one place. It's similar to the situations in London or Amsterdam, but a contradiction to these cities at the same time. London and Amsterdam keep traditions but New York is not shaped by heavy cultural traditions. So while English traditions and manners shape London, New York has a kind of openness.

Is there anything about New York that took time to get used to?

There is this subway kind of attitude: you are part of a crowd and on your own at the same time. People are very private here in New York. You can see how people try to kind of protect their own energy and privacy. That's something I've noticed. It's also the fact that people very rarely invite you home to their apartments. If you know people and they are having a birthday party, they will invite you, but it's always at bars. I remember the first time when someone invited me to a birthday party. It was a girl I was working with. She gave me an address and I thought it was for her place. But it turned out to be a bar.

What is it about New York that you miss when you're abroad?

New York has the best variety of restaurants. I always miss Asian food when I am not in New York.

Where do you go to get the best Asian food?

To *Joe's Shanghai*. They have really amazing soup dumplings. And there is another place I like to go to. It's called *Nyonya*. It's a good Malaysian restaurant. And if you only want to spend a little money, I suggest going to the *Hong Kong Supermarket* on Hester Street. In there you can buy really good sushi for almost no money.

And when it comes to healthy food?

Then there is no other than *Souen*.

Jeppe Hein's installation "All We Need Is Inside" at 303 Gallery

And something typical like burgers?
You shouldn't miss *Lovely Day.*

And coffee?
I only drink coffee at home. I am not a coffee-to-go person.

Where do you live?
In Chinatown.

What is the neighbourhood like?
It's very central; it's right next to SoHo. The Lower East side has always attracted artists. But this is changing now because the spaces that were here ten years ago— all the loft spaces—have all been converted into rental units. It's almost impossible to find a studio here. It's a very dense neighbourhood. I think it's an inspiring neighbourhood because you can choose to be left alone. And I think that's also what I want to say about New York City, in general: if you walk the streets in Europe wearing sunglasses, it's almost too much. It's kind of like playing out an attitude. Maybe it's even unfriendly. It feels like you are being pretentious, especially in Denmark where I am from, where we like the light. It's the completely opposite in New York. There, putting sunglasses on is nonchalant. People wouldn't look at you. And it's practical. If I feel stressed out and have to go by subway, I wear my sunglasses just to get a little bit of peace. I even see people in my gym wearing sunglasses. Or people in restaurants who sit by themselves. You constantly wonder what a person is up to or what they do. Europe is a flat society. People very much have the same expression and look. The diversity of characters in New York is so widespread. It provides privacy.

Sounds mysterious.
It is. There are so many people living in Chinatown whose culture I am not familiar with and it's hard

Russian wellness temple in Coney Island: Mermaid Spa

to learn about it. I have been living here for eight years and I still don't know what's going on. A lot of people here don't speak English. The communication is really scaled out to the minimum. This is very fascinating to me. And visually, it's also a very interesting place to live.

You live on Hester Street, which is also the title of one of your series. What is the connection?

It's a Chinese street. It went well with the work I was doing as I was trying not to bind it to something too specific. It's kind of left to interpretation. And that's exactly what Chinatown is for me, too. It's something that moves really fast and it's kind of complicated to understand. There are a lot of details but it's really hard to come up with a conclusion.

Is the city of New York an inspiration for you too?

Yes, for its openness, diversity and complexity. In fact, everything —not just in one way, and that's what inspires me. But my sources of inspiration aren't necessarily big issues like neighbourhoods or cities. For my latest drawings, for example, I got inspired by the floor of my bathroom. So I am exploring both my micro and macrocosmos. And I think that fits me very well.

What's your favourite gallery in New York City?

Untitled Gallery on Orchard Street is a good one. And there is *Off Vendome*. There's a German guy running it; he also has a space in Dusseldorf and just opened up another one in New York City. I was really impressed by the program. When I was there, there was a drawing show on display. It was inspiring. I am also very much into sculptures. For that, I like to go to *303 Gallery*. They have some nice artists expressing sculptural works. I also like *Andrea Rosen*

Gallery. It has a great program too. And there is also a gallery called *Old Room*. It's a gallery, but it's in an apartment located in the Meatpacking District.

There are also the big ones, like Gagosian.
Oh yes, *Gagosian, Zwirner*—I like them too. The gallery world in Chelsea is so wealthy. They show the most accomplished artists in the world.

Which museums do you like?
The *MoMa*. A little bit more conservative, but still interesting.

Is there currently an art movement you observe?
Book publishing has a very great influence, so people keep producing their very own small zines and books. But that trend has already been running for a while. It's a nice opportunity to bypass traditional gallery settings in order to show your works, create your own publicity.

Is there a New York-based artist whom you admire?
Yes, but this changes quite quickly. At the moment I am very much into Barry X Ball. I am fascinated by his sculptures.

Is New York really the city that never sleeps?
Yes, it's fascinating to think about all the stuff you can do here.

What would you never miss out on?
Events that I go to to support people's work. Mostly exhibitions. And some events are just important for networking.

Where do you go out?
I never go to clubs, as I can't stand the aesthetics. I don't like the way clubs play with hierarchy;

I like things that are accessible to everyone—where you don't have to line up and fear the doorman. I like to go to karaoke bars. I go there with a couple of friends and it's so funny.

Where do you go to relax?
My favourite places to go to are Coney Island and Brighton Beach. If it's winter, you can take the subway out to Coney Island and go the Russian sauna there. It's called *Mermaid Spa*. There you can spend the whole day, use the sauna and eat Russian food. But I also like to go there in the summer when you can walk down to Brighton Beach. It's a Russian neighbourhood and you can get really great Russian food there: fish, salad—it's very raw and fresh. It's like a Russian community. They don't actually speak too much English.

So it's a bit like Chinatown again?
I guess I like to be left alone. I like to observe people.

Where would you take a guest visiting you for 38 hours?
I would definitely recommend people to go to Times Square. But it would be without me. I can't stand the place. Then I would join them again to go on the Staten Island ferry. It's free and it gives you a great view of the city. It's kind of romantic. Prospect Park is also nice to go to. And of course, the beach. Far Rockaway is a nice place. You can go there by train; it takes about an hour.

Inside the latest David Zwirner Gallery space designed by Annabelle Selldorf.

East Side Story

Beyond the concentration of the rich and famous, and their brigades of doormen, butlers and chauffeurs, this once WASP-only enclave is going through a renaissance and remains to some as the only authentic neighbourhood left in the city.

| Shop · Food · Culture | The Gold Coast |

Often referred to as the 'Gold Coast' of shopping, Madison Avenue is Fifth Avenue's chicer, more sophisticated sister. Nowhere else will you find this concentration of shopping emporiums. From new kids on the block *Proenza Schouler*'s David Adjaye-designed flagship (photo) to old guard *Ralph Lauren's Rhinelander Mansion*, Madison Avenue has it all. *Barneys*, located at the Upper East Side's southern edge, set the standard for the cool,

upscale department store, which to this day continues to live up to its reputation. While you're looking at the latest offerings from *Celine* or *Tom Ford*, don't forget to drop into *Viand* for its legendary turkey sandwich, and catch a peek of the latest on view at the uptown *Gagosian* gallery. Madison Avenue exudes timeless elegance with contemporary flair; a distinctively New York experience.

• Upper East Side, several locations, see index p. 67

American Standard

Ralph Lauren epitomises American luxury. His new restaurant fills in the blank space of his resumé. The native New Yorker has reimagined the former La Cote Basque into his vision of timeless, sophisticated, American elegance. The clubby atmosphere, replete with coffered ceilings, tartan pillows, leather banquettes and the requisite equestrian theme are all present and accounted for. The menu consists of fine renditions of straightforward American classics: a perfect iceberg wedge, a salty satisfying bacon cheeseburger, and—a nod to his Bronx roots—corned-beef-and-Swiss on rye.
• The Polo Bar, 1 East 55th Street, Upper East Side, ralphlauren.com

Outdoors   The Secret Garden

If Central Park is said to be the jewel in the crown that is New York City, then it could be said that the *Conservatory Garden* is its most elegant facet. Divided into three distinct styles—English, French and Italian—this six-acre allocation is the park's formal garden. The garden recalls an era that novelist Edith Wharton dubbed 'The Age of Innocence': the 19th-century reign of the East Coast upper class. The magnificent Iron gate that marks the main entrance originally stood before the Vanderbilt Mansion. An officially designated quiet zone; it makes for a welcome respite during a hectic tour.
• Central Park Conservatory Garden, Fifth Ave. at 105th Street, Upper East Side, centralparknyc.org

Food   Down to Earth

EJ's Luncheonette, which we New York natives affectionately call EJ's, is an Upper East Side institution. EJ's has stood the test of time and finicky palates—it's not fancy, it doesn't try to be, and it is consistently delicious. Step into a NYC diner with a retro feel and get cozy on their blue leather banquettes. Their brunch menu is extensive, savoury and sweet, who can say no to fluffy pancakes or indulgent omelettes? If you miss brunch, don't worry—head over for a cheeseburger and fries. It would be mistake to leave EJ's without getting a milkshake!
• EJ's Luncheonette, 1271 3rd Ave., Upper East Side, ejsluncheonette.com

La Dolce Vita

Manhattan has always benefited from being a town built by immigrants. One of the benefits of such a history is the influx of a rich culinary tradition from around the globe. The Upper East side is the home to many fine eateries, and Italian cuisine takes pride of place—Milanese to be exact. Before shopping or after a museum, make sure to drop into *Sant Ambroeus* or *Via Quadronno*. Sant Ambroeus, which opened in 1936, is a celebrated pasticceria and confetteria as well as being a destination for Manhattan's gelato connoisseurs. Via Quadronno is famous not only for its paninis, but also for its cappuccinos and homemade pastries.
• Upper East Side, several locations, see Index p. 67

Shop Salon Setting

In these days of high-street fast fashion and mega-brand flagship stores, very few retail salons remain. *Yuta Powell* has chosen to harken back to the 1930s, 40s and 50s when most design houses chose to show their clothing in an actual showroom setting. Mentored by none other than Hubert de Givenchy himself, Yuta Powell's distinct eye is geared toward those that appreciate style over fashion, elegance over ostentation. In an atmosphere that's more intimate than intimidating, it's as if a very stylish friend has asked you to stop by to look at some unique and interesting things.
• Yuta Powell, 19 East 75th Street, Upper East Side, yutapowell.com

Night Presidential Cocktail

Socialites, politicians, movie stars and moguls have all bellied up to *Bemelmans Bar*. From chocolate brown leather banquettes to white-jacketed waiters, to a 24-karat gold leafed ceiling, this elegant boîte boasts the discreet charm of the bourgeoisie dipped in Art Deco splendour. Named for Ludwig Bemelman, the creator of the classic Madeline children's books, it also hosts the only surviving Bemelmans' commission open to the public. Settle into a single malt while taking comfort in knowing that it's a fraction of the cost of Café Carlyle across the hall.
• Bemelmans Bar, The Carlyle Hotel, 35 East 76th Street, Upper East Side, rosewoodhotels.com

Culture | **History Conserved**

Founded by the Pittsburgh coal and steel industrialist Henry Clay Frick, *The Frick Collection* evokes the splendor and tranquility of the Gilded Age. At the time of his death, Mr. Frick bequeathed his New York residence and the most outstanding of his many artworks to establish a public gallery for the purpose of 'encouraging and developing the study of the fine arts'. The Frick Collection now houses a permanent collection of more than 1,100 works of art from the Renaissance to the late nineteenth century. The Frick, as it's simply known by locals, is not only museum, but a grand former residence. From the domestic atmosphere, the filtered natural light,

the varying ambiance you experience from room to room, the strict rules, and, most importantly, the finely curated artworks hanging on the walls, you could travel the world and it would be difficult to visit any museum more satisfying than The Frick. There is just enough to see and experience within a single visit, as the entire collection can be viewed within less than two hours. Both the mansion and the works within it serve as a monument to one of America's greatest art collectors.
• The Frick Collection, 1 East 70th Street, Upper East Side, frick.org

Manhattan Munchies

Maya & Dean Jankelowitz
The couple run Jack's Wife Freda, a SoHo-based bistro with American-Mediterranean cooking. Maya from Israel and Dean from South-Africa met while working at Balthazar. The couple now bring bits of their respective personal backgrounds to the kitchen in their shared space. Having eaten out in the city for more than 15 years, and having worked in some of the greatest city restaurants, the pair know the NYC food scene from the ground up. Maya and Dean now have two boys and live in Manhattan.

Following the culinary path laid out by Maya and Dean we'll learn that NYC's best pastrami sandwich is still served in a classic spot, while the best burger joint is hidden in the back of a hotel. The couple loves the classics and will take us on a tour from spacious, early morning brunch places to shadowy bars for a few late-night drinks.

Serving Middle Eastern Food since 1971: Mamoun's Falafel Restaurant.

There are a lot of things happening on the other side of East River—is Manhattan yesterday's concept?

Maya: Definitely not! Manhattan was, is and will always be the new world!

Dean: It's why we came here; it's what we want to experience. Naturally people live in the other boroughs by circumstance or choice, but Manhattan will always be the heart.

Where is the heat in Manhattan today?

Maya: We think anything between Canal Street up to 14th Street (and from the East river to the Hudson) is always going to be cool, interesting and innovative. We are very local, and find NY to be like a village—so whatever is local for you feels up and and coming.

Speaking of the NYC restaurant scene, which is the best in your opinion? Where do you go to eat out?

Maya: We like classics, anything that's been open for awhile. We usually fear walking into a new restaurant—our expectations are often not met.

Dean: We love *Cafe Mogador*, *Cafe Gitane*, and *Strip House*. For something unusual we go to *Amaranth* on the Upper East Side, *Blue Ribbon Sushi*, and *Blue Ribbon Bakery*. *Lure FishBar* is our recommendation for a spacious brunch with kids. We like *Gemma*, *The Odeon*, anything owned by Danny Meyer, and of course *Jack's Wife Freda*—our own restaurant.

Maya: And you will find us at our neighbouring restaurant where Dean and I love to escape to: *Sant Ambroeus SoHo* on Lafayette Street. It's just a block away from

Jack's Wife Freda. We go there for the pasta and we feel so comfortable because of Alireza the maitre. We usually escape there to do office work, but it always feels like a special occasion when we go.

Pastrami sandwiches, hamburgers, clam chowder… NYC has its traditional food. Do you have recommendations—besides the touristy spots—for a solid old-school experience?

Maya: For pastrami sandwiches we obviously go to *Katz's Deli*. We live a couple blocks away, and we love sitting with all the tourists. The truth is, you can't beat Katz's.

Dean: We love the burger in the hidden burger joint in the *Parker Meridien Hotel*. Also, I recently had the burger at *Peter Luger* for the first time—and it definitely gets all the press for a very good reason.

Which traditional dish should I not miss and where can I get it?

Maya: Shawarma at *Mamoun's Falafel Restaurant* on Macdougal Street by Washington Square Park.

Dean: The curry laksa noodle soup at *Kelley & Ping* in SoHo.

NYC is famous for its mix of cultures. What are the cuisines which take you to a trip far away from home?

Maya: It's beyond restaurants; you can feel it in the streets. I love Chinatown. We have Little Italy on Mulberry Street, Koreatown on 32th street, St. Marks for little Tel Aviv, Murray hill and Curry hill, Astoria Queens for authentic Greek food—I love *Elias Corner*, they have the best Greek salad.

NY is also a bar town. What are your three favourite bars?

Maya: *Forget Me Not* on Division Street and *Milano's Bar* on Houston.

Dean: I also like the *Spring Lounge* on Spring Street.

What are the interesting food markets in the city I should visit?

Maya: There is the *Farmers Market in Union Square*. Also nice is *Eataly* in the Flatiron district on 23rd Street.

Dean: Or *Chelsea Market*…

You have kids… What is best activity on a sunny NYC day with the little ones?

Maya: We have a picnic in Central Park, with a stroll, boat ride and zoo visit all in one outing.

Dean: And we love walking the streets to see where we end up.

Hidden behind the curtain in the atrium lobby of Le Parker Meridien hotel: The Burger Joint.

New York City Survival Kit

Shady Business

In New York, they're not necessarily used to block out the sun, but as our collaborator, Asger Carlsen, notes sunglasses are a fine way "to get a little bit of peace". Go to Silver Lining to pick up a pair from their own designs or the vintage leather frames you always wanted.
• Silver Lining, silverliningopticians.com

Walk of Shame

There are mornings in New York when people don't necessarily wake up in their own bed. If you find yourself in need of freshening up, you can pick up Poppy Rouge or any other scent from D.S and Durga developed in a studio in Gowanus, Brooklyn.
• D.S & Durga, dsanddurga.com

Urban Liquor Pioneers

Getting mellow in New York is always a unique experience. This Bourbon is described as "exotic and deep, with flavors of grain, licorice, vanilla and molasses" (Eric Asimov, New York Times). It's produced locally in an old Brooklyn Navy Yard by Kings County Distillery which is New York City's oldest operating whiskey distillery—founded in 2010—and the first founded after Prohibition.
• Bourbon, Kings County Distillery, kingscountydistillery.com

Books

Bright Lights, Big City
• Jay McInerney, 1984

Mid-town New York City in the 1980s. A novel about a life in the fast lane. Cocaine, clubs and a tragic hero who's in love with a supermodel. The main character, who remains unnamed struggles to get a handle on his life filled with vice, and seeks redemption in surprising places.

Goodbye To All That
• Joan Didion, 1967

In her essay, California native Didion explains why she left her adoptive home of New York at the age of 28, where she was living as a struggling writer. It's a terrific insight into New York of the 1960s where writers could afford centrally located Manhattan apartments but would have to, as Didion says, "charge food at Bloomingdale's gourmet shop in order to eat".

Joe Gould's Secret
• Joseph Mitchell, 1965

In the form of two New Yorker articles written by Mitchell, Joe Gould's secret follows an eccentric psychiatric patient and Harvard graduate from a distinguished family who's spent his nights wandering the taverns of Greenwich Village. Allegedly working on his masterpiece An Oral History of Our Time, the line between reality and fiction is somewhat blurred in this introspective work

Films

Ciao! Manhattan
• John Palmer, David Weisman, 1972

She was the most intriguing of Warhol's so-called superstars but throughout her short life she was plummeting into an abyss. The documentary shows Edie Sedgwick as the queen of Manhattan, lover, and junkie.

Wild Style
• Charlie Ahearn, 1982

Back in the times when New York was a rough and unpredictable playground, this movie captures a moment in time when Hip Hop and spraycan art were in their earliest days. Starring Grandmaster Flash, Rocksteady Crew, Fab Five Freddy, the film boasts a killer soundtrack.

Mean Streets
• Martin Scorsese, 1973

Scorsese's third feature film, made with a 500k budget, documents the life of two low-level gangsters (De Niro and Keitel). Rolling Stones tunes are perfectly placed to set the mood of the film, which acts as an on-point insight into the director's native 1960s Little Italy.

Music

Dinosaur L
• 24–24 Music, 1982

Arthur Russell is the genius behind Dinosaur L. From experimental compositions to collaboration with the Talking Heads or Bootsy Collins, he also contributed several club anthems which were floorfillers in clubs like Paradise Garage and The Loft. This album shows the early works of Russell and features the uber-track Go Bang.

Fireworks XII: 3 Documentaries
• John Zorn, 2002

Originally from the Lower East Side, John Zorn gets his inspiration from the diverse nature of his surroundings. In this LP originally written as the score for three documentary films, he fuses several styles which embody the eclecticism of the streets of NY.

Songs for Distingué Lovers
• Billie Holiday, 1957

Throughout her short life, Billie wandered from tragedy to excess, and this late record of 1957 hints at her personal struggle and breakdown. A perfect piece for deep and sentimental New York nights.

The Ludlow Hotel

Imagine New York of the 1980s with its tremendous art, early hip hop, and punk rock scenes. Then translate that vitality to a hotel on the Lower East Side. Put together you get The Ludlow Hotel. The stunning result is seen as soon as you walk through the steel and glass doors of the lobby into a lounge with oak-paneled walls, antique chandeliers, and Parisian- and New Orleans-inspired craft cocktails. The 184 rooms have a lofty industrial vibe with big casement windows, furry throws on chairs, and lavish bathrooms. And the hotel's eagerly awaited restaurant, Dirty French, serves Gallic classics with a New York sensibility.

Book now on 38hrs.com

Advertorial

The Jane Hotel

Built in 1907 as a lodging house for seamen, The Jane Hotel has since been tastefully renovated and offers a 99$-a-night economic hideout for a stay in the city. The Cafe Gitane restaurant, Ballroom and rooftop bar are fine spots to mingle with the local population. The "cabins" are compact and well equipped, some offer views of the Hudson River. The bath is where it always throughout the years, down the hall.

Book now on 38hrs.com

A Burglar's Complaint

Lawrence Block

So I took the subway to Union Square and walked a couple of blocks to a storefront on East Eleventh Street, where a tailless cat dozed in the window. Inside I found Bernie Rhodenbarr perched on a stool behind the counter, reading the latest Wallace Stroby novel.

"It's about Crissa Stone," my favorite bookseller announced. "A professional thief. Sort of like Richard Stark's Parker, but without a Y chromosome. I'll tell you, it makes me miss the old days."

"When men were men?"

"When it was possible for an enterprising individual to make money the old-fashioned way."

"By working for it?"

He shook his head. "By stealing it. And I'm not talking about computer crime and identity theft and all of that sneaky cyber-stuff. I mean leaving one's own house and letting oneself into somebody else's. I mean breaking and entering—and then exiting richer than when you entered. I mean picking locks and jimmying doors and outfoxing doormen and elevator operators."

"You mean burglary."

"Once," he said, "it was a profession. A morally reprehensible one, I'll grant you, but one with a set of standards and a code of ethics and a steep learning curve, designed to separate the sheep from the goats, the ribbon from the clerks, and the fool from his money. And what is it now?"

"I don't know," I said, "but I have a feeling you're about to tell me."

"A fool's errand," he said. "I have two trades, burglary and bookselling. That's two sets of footprints in the sands of time, and I wouldn't encourage any son of mine to follow in either of them."

"You don't have a son," I pointed out.

"And a good thing," he said, "because what kind of a role model would I be? Two careers, and both of them victims of the twenty-first century."

"Oh?"

"Nobody buys books anymore," he said. "For that I blame technology, whether it's e-books or the Internet."

"People still steal," I said.

"And get caught, because you can't walk a block without getting your picture taken half a dozen times. There are security cameras everywhere, up and down every street and inside of most large buildings. Do you know

what I did last Thursday?"

"No idea."

"Well, you would," he said, "if you looked at the right tapes. I went to an address in the East Sixties, where a supermodel whose name you would recognize uses a dresser drawer for what ought to be in a safe-deposit box."

"Jewelry?"

"Her building's a brownstone," he said, "so there's no doorman, no onsite security people. And she was in St. Croix, shooting a spread for the Sports Illustrated Swimsuit issue, so the house was empty."

"Except for her jewelry."

"And other valuables. I went there and I stood out in front of her building. I was close enough to see the lock on the front door, and I figured it would take me about thirty seconds to pick it. I waited while the sky darkened, and the programmed lights went on in some of the rooms." He sighed. "I had a brown paper bag in my pocket."

"To hold the loot?"

"To pull over my head. I'd already cut eye holes in the thing."

"So the cameras wouldn't trip you up."

"But what good would it do? They'd check cameras on the street, and find images of me before I put the bag over my head. Or, even if I got out of a cab with my head already in the bag, there'd be footage from the day before, when I cased the site. So I walked home."

"You walked?"

"Through Central Park. It's a pleasant route, but there may have been security cameras in the trees, taking note of my presence. If so, there's probably a picture of me taking the paper bag out of my pocket and dropping it in a trashcan."

"At least you didn't litter."

"I wouldn't dare," he said. "Not these days, in this city." In the window, his cat stretched and yawned. "Smile, Raffles," he told it. "For the camera."

Lawrence Block is a serial offender, his weapon is the typewriter. He's written over 100 crime stories and won several prices including "The Edgar Allen Poe Award". Block is best known for the New York-set series about the detective Matthew Scudder and the gentleman burglar Bernie Rhodenbarr. The movie "A Walk Among the Tombstones" from 2014, starring Liam Neeson as Matthew Scudder, is based on one of Block's novels.

Available from 38HOURS

Issue No.1   **38HOURSin**   English edition

BERLiN BERLiN BERLiN

Art in a WWII bunker, fashion in a hidden warehouse, nouvelle Deutsch cuisine on the canal, biking on a historic airstrip, cocktails beneath a giant rocket... Discover the city of reinvention in 38 hours.

Issue No.2   **38HOURSin**   English edition

Paris Paris Paris Paris

A hidden vineyard in Montmartre, an African bar along the Canal, new French cuisine on the Rive Droite, breathtaking views from a rooftop bar in Ménilmontant... Discover the Parisian "renouveau" in 38 hours.

Issue No.3   **38HOURSin**   English edition

Amster dam Amster dam Amster dam

Artist studios in churches, a hidden bar in a burger joint, hippie beaches in the center, a restaurant in a greenhouse, thrilling views from the old docks ... Discover an Amsterdam beyond canals and coffeeshops in 38 hours.

Issue No.4   **38HOURSin**   English edition

LON DON LON DON

A Michelin starred pub, a super-secret bar, a book club with a massive sound system. A quiet green hill to behold the city's skyline and a nighttime restaurant above the clouds... Discover an evolving London in 38 hours.

Issue No.5   **38HOURSin**   English edition

Vienna Vienna Vienna

A secret café with an impressive vinyl collection, a disco ball pizza oven, a cemetery for the nameless, a restaurant in an old Apotheke and Europe's finest tap water... Discover Vienna from Schubert to Falco in 38 hours.

Issue No.6   **38HOURSin**   English edition

Milan Milan Milan

A flamingo garden, slow food markets, a secret bar, traditional trattorias, hidden masterpieces of Italian design... Discover the ever changing city of Milan in 38 hours.

Issue No.7   **38HOURSin**   English edition

BARCE LONA BARCE LONA

Tapas with a modern twist, utopian housing projects, thrilling views from a diving board, art spaces in abandoned factories, broad beaches in the outskirts... Discover the Barcelona beyond the Ramblas in 38 hours.

Issue No.8   **38HOURSin**   English edition

NYC NYC NYC

Tropical vibes in Queens, Michelin starred viking cuisine, ice-cold Martinis in Kennedy's haunt, Brooklyn handcrafted jeans, beach life with The Boss, dolce vita in the Bronx... Discover the sparkling city of New York in 38 hours.

Next Issue: Stockholm

WWW.38HRS.COM

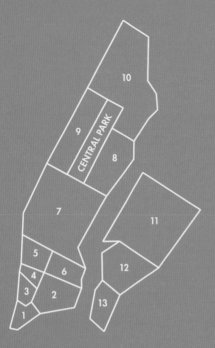

5/West Village

Blue Ribbon bakery
35 Downing St
+1 212 337 0404
blueribbonrestaurants
.com → p. 53 Ⓕ

Bond 07 by Selima
7 Bond St
+1 212 677 8487
selimaoptique.com
→ p.16 Ⓢ

Bond Street
6 Bond St
+1 212 777 2500
bondstrestaurant.com
→ p.15 Ⓕ

Casa
72 Bedford St
+1 212 366 9410
casarestaurant.com
→ p.16 Ⓕ

Casa Magazines
22 8th Ave
+1 212 645 1197
→ p.33 Ⓢ

Fat Radish
17 Orchard St
+1 212 300 4053
thefatradishnyc.com
→ p.15 Ⓕ

Jivamukti Café
841 Broadway
+1 212 353 0214
jivamukteacafe.com
→ p.15 Ⓕ

Kelley & Ping
127 Greene St
+1 212 228 1212
kelleyandping.com
→ p.54 Ⓕ

La Taza de Oro
96 8th Ave
+1 212 243 9946
→ p.16 Ⓕ

Lure FishBar
142 Mercer St
+1 212 431 7676
lurefishbar.com
→ p. 53 Ⓕ

Mamoun's Falafel Restaurant
119 Macdougal St
+1 212 674 8685
mamouns.com
→ p.54 Ⓕ

Milano's Bar
51 E Houston St
+1 212 226 8844
→ p.54 Ⓝ

Minetta Tavern
113 Macdougal St
+1 212 475 3850
minettatavernny.com
→ p.15 Ⓝ

Oak
28 Bond St
+1 212 677 1293
oaknyc.com
→ p.16 Ⓢ

Old Room
675 Hudson
old-room.com
→ Ⓒ

Poisson Rouge
158 Bleecker St
+1 212 505 3474
lepoissonrouge.com
→ p.14 Ⓕ

SoHo House
29–35 9th Ave
+1 212 627 9800
SoHohouseny.com
→ p.32 Ⓝ

Spring Lounge
48 Spring St
+1 212 965 1774
thespringlounge.com
→ p.54 Ⓝ

Stella Dallas
218 Thompson St
+1 212 674 0447
→ p.33 Ⓢ

Strip House
11 E 12th St
+1 212 838 9197
striphouse.com
→ p. 53 Ⓕ

Sunsets-Jane Hotel
113 Jane St
+1 212 924 6700
thejanenyc.com
→ p.9 Ⓝ

Zinc Bar
82 W 3rd Street
+1 212 477 9462
zincbar.com
→ p.16 Ⓝ

6/East Village

9th Street Community Garden
9th street
communitygarden
softheeastvillage.com
→ p.10 Ⓞ

A1 records
439 E 6th St
+1 212 473 2870
a1recordshop.com
→ p.24 Ⓢ

Cafe Mogador
101 St Marks Pl
+1 212 677 2226
cafemogador.com
→ p. 53 Ⓕ

City Cinemas Village East
181 Second Avenue
+1 212 529 6998
villageeastcinema.com
→ p.33 Ⓒ

Gemma
335 Bowery
+1 212 505 7300
theboweryhotel.com
→ p.53 Ⓕ

Katz's Deli
205 E Houston St
+1 212 254 2246
katzsdelicatessen.com
→ p.54 Ⓕ, Ⓢ

Kyo Ya
94 E 7th St
+1 212 982 4140
→ Ⓕ

Momofuku
207 2nd Ave
+1 212 254 3500
momofuku.com
→ p.24 Ⓕ

Souen
326 E 6th St
+1 212 388 1155
souen.net
→ p.43 Ⓕ

The Strand Bookstore
828 Broadway
+1 212 473 1452
strandbooks.com
→ p.24 Ⓢ

7/Midtown

303 Gallery
507 W 24th St
+1 212 255 1121
303gallery.com
→ p.45 Ⓒ

Andrea Rosen Gallery
525 W 24th St
+1 212 627 6000
andrearosengallery
.com → p.46 Ⓒ

Bergdorf Goodman
754 5th Ave
bergdorfgoodman.com
→ p.32 Ⓢ

Bruce Silverstein
535 W 24th St
+1 212 627 3930
brucesilverstein.com
→ Ⓒ

Burger Joint in the Parker Meridien Hotel
119 W 56th St
+1 212 708 7414
parkermeridien.com
→ p.54 Ⓕ

Cook Shop
156 10th Ave
+1 212 924 4440
cookshopny.com
→ p.15 Ⓕ

Eataly
200 Fifth Avenue
+1 212 229 2560
eataly.com
→ p.54 Ⓕ, Ⓢ

Gagosian
555 W 24th St
+1 212 741 1111
gagosian.com
→ p.46 Ⓒ

Joe's Shanghai
24 W 56th St
joeshanghairestau
rants.com
→ p.43 Ⓕ

Keens
72 W 36th St
+1 212 947 3636
keens.com
→ p.11 Ⓕ

La Luncheonette
130 10th Ave
+1 212 675 0342
→ p.15 Ⓕ

Moma
11 W 53rd St
+1 212 708 9400
moma.org
→ p.46 Ⓒ

Off Vendome
254 W 23rd #2
offvendome.de
→ p.45 Ⓒ

Allswell
124 Bedford Ave
+1 347 799 2743
allswellnyc.tumblr.com
→ p. 24 Ⓕ, Ⓝ

Amarcord
252 Lafayette St # A
+1 212 431 4161
amarcordvintage
fashion.com
→ p. 33 Ⓢ

Artists & Fleas
70 N 7th St
+1 917 488 4203
artistsandfleas.com
→ p. 33 Ⓢ

Black Brick
300 Bedford Ave
+1 718 384 0075
→ p. 33 Ⓕ

**Brooklyn Museum
and Botanical Gardens**
200 Eastern Parkway
+1 718 638 5000
brooklynmuseum.org
→ p.16 Ⓒ

Crown Victoria
60 S 2nd St
+1 917 719 6072
crownvicbar.com
→ p.15 Ⓝ

Hotel Delmano
82 Berry St
+1 718 387 1945
hoteldelmano.com
→ p.15 Ⓝ

IF
94 Grand St
+1 212 334 4964
ifSoHonewyork.com
→ p.16 Ⓢ

Marlow and Sons
81 Broadway
+1 718 384 1441
marlowandsons.com
→ p.15 Ⓕ

Mary Meyer Vintage
56 Bogart St
+1 718 386 6279
marymeyerclothing
.com
→ p.16 Ⓢ

Output Club
74 Wythe Ave
outputclub.com
→ p. 24, 32 Ⓝ

Peter Luger
178 Broadway
+1 718 387 7400
peterluger.com
→ p.11, 54 Ⓕ

Peter Luger Steakhouse
178 Broadway
+1 718 387 7400
peterluger.com
→ p.11 Ⓕ

Rye
247 S 1st St
+1 718 218 8047
ryerestaurant.com
→ p.32 Ⓕ

Sheltering Sky
160 N 12th St
+1 718 218 7500
chelseahotels.com
→ p.9 Ⓝ

Smorgasbord
90 Kent Ave
smorgasburg.com
→ p.16 Ⓞ

Tabare
221 S 1st St
+1 347 335 0187
tabarenyc.com
→ p.15 Ⓕ

The Diner
85 Broadway
+1 718 486 3077
dinernyc.com
→ p.14 Ⓕ

Verboten
54 N 11th St
verbotennewyork.com
→ p.24 Ⓝ

Whythe Hotel
80 Wythe Ave
+1 718 460 8000
wythehotel.com
→ p.15 Ⓞ

Woodhull
644 Driggs Ave
+1 718 387 9463
woodhulwinebar.com
→ p.32 Ⓝ

0/Outskirts

**Arthur Avenue
Retail Market**
2321 Hughes Ave
+1 347 590 6711
arthuravenue.com
→ p.8 Ⓢ

Borgatti's
632 E 187th St
+1 718 367 3799
borgattis.com
→ p.8 Ⓢ, Ⓕ

Botanical Garden
2900 Southern Blvd
+1 718 817 8700
nybg.org
→ p.8 Ⓞ

Calabria
2338 Arthur Ave
+1 718 367 5145
n.e → p.8 Ⓕ

Di Fara
1424 Avenue J
+1 718 258 1367
difara.com
→ p.15 Ⓕ

**Franklin D Roosevelt
Memorial**
1 FDR Four
Freedoms Park
+1 212 204 8831
fdrfourfreedomspark
.org → Ⓒ

Mermaid Spa
3703 Mermaid Avenue
+1 347 462 2166
seagatebaths.com
→ p.46 Ⓞ

Momo
43 Bogart St
+1 718 418 6666
momosushishack.com
→ p.15 Ⓕ

Nathan's
569 Myrtle Ave
+1 718 783 3744
→ p.15 Ⓕ

Porta
911 Kingsley St
+1 732 776 7661
pizzaporta.com
→ p.17 Ⓕ

Roberta's Pizza
261 Moore St
+1 718 417 1118
robertaspizza.com
→ p.15, 24 Ⓕ

Roberto's
603 Crescent Ave
+1 718 733 9503
robertos.roberto089
.com → p.8 Ⓕ

The River Café
1 Water St
+1 718 522 5200
therivercafe.com
→ p.15 Ⓕ

Tra Di Noi
622 E 187th St
+1 718 295 1784
tradinoi.com
→ p.8 Ⓕ

BON VOYAGE

38HOURS offers a handpicked selection of city trips throughout Europe.

Your perfect city trip: Online, by mail or by phone – we individually handle your booking inquiry – from flights, hotels to restaurant reservations. Receive insider information and your personal itinerary with handpicked recommendations tailored to your desires. Our selection of experiences ranges from independent boutiques, galleries, neighborhood bars to brand new restaurants. Experience a new city from within.

Book your next city trip on:

WWW.38HRS.COM

ON THE ROAD

The App for the Discerning Traveller

Explore insider recommendations and create your personal itinerary with handpicked locations tailored to your desires. Our selection of experiences ranges from independent boutiques, galleries, neighborhood bars to brand new restaurants. Experience a new city from within.

38 HOURS